Estate Planning

The Basics

Step-By-Step

Planning Your Estate

Neil Bryan, MBA

Book 5: Money Action Plan Series

Revised & Updated 2023 version

Estate Planning – The Basics

Copyright 2016-2023 Neil Edward Bryan

Published by The Neimaur Group LLC

ISBN: 978-1539081579

All rights reserved. No part of this book may be used or reproduced in any manner whatsoever without written permission except in the case of brief quotations embodied in articles and reviews.

Estate Planning – The Basics

Dedication

To Maureen

Estate Planning – The Basics

Disclaimer

This book is intended to help you prepare your information and financial data to have a constructive meeting with an estate attorney.

Although I have a Bachelor's degree and a Master's in Business Administration (MBA) and have worked for over forty years in the financial industry, please note that **I am not an attorney so the information in this book regarding estate planning should not be considered as legal advice.**

Contents

Introduction 1
What You Will Learn..7
Getting Ready 9
Terminology...15
Components of an Estate Plan 31
What you must decide..37
Methods of transferring your assets 45
Meeting with Your Estate Attorney 55
For What It's Worth...59
Forms for Estate Planning....................................63
How can the Money Action Plan Software help you with your Estate Plan?...................................75
Conclusion 77
About the Author 79
Other Neil Bryan Books.......................................81
Neil Bryan WEBSITES: 85
Neil Bryan Software..87

Estate Planning – The Basics

Introduction

Why I Wrote This Book

This is the fifth book in the Money Action Plan series. This process uses step by step instructions to lead the reader through the sometimes-intricate world of personal finance and simplify the process for everyone.

Experienced estate planners will find this fourth book has basic information and is not for them. While I welcome feedback on the book, please be aware of the basic aspects of the book and abstain from a review if the review is simply stating that the book only presents basic information. This is what the book is intended to do.

The estate planning process documented in this book is personal. What this means is that it is the process I used to get my estate ready to be sure my wishes will be fulfilled after my death.

Why You Should Read This Book

This book continues where the first four books in the series left off.

The first book, *Budgeting and Money Management – The Basics*, presented the reader with basic budgeting and money management techniques aided by the Money Action Plan software available with the purchase of the book.

The second book, *Keep More of What You Earn*, presented a more detailed approach to reviewing and maximizing your income and reviewing and minimizing your expenses.

The third book, *Investing – The Basics*, presented a step-by-step approach for getting started in investing.

The fourth book, *Retirement Planning - The Basics*, presented a step-by-step approach to planning for your retirement.

In this fifth book, we will simplify the process of planning your estate. We will look at what estate planning means as compared to retirement planning and give you the information you will need to help you make the decisions that have to be made in order to be ready when the time comes. Using this approach, you will be able to make the proper decisions about planning your estate.

Also, as with the first four books, the Money Action Plan software and the NEW Estate Planning Software are available to help with this but is not necessary for success in planning your estate.

Additional DISCLAIMER:

In case you missed it on the Disclaimer page, please note that **I am not an attorney so the information in this book regarding estate planning should not be considered as legal advice.**

As in my previous books, I will tell you what I know and researched about the topic of estate planning and what I have done in my personal life regarding planning my estate, but the ***actual planning of your estate should be done in conjunction with a qualified estate planning attorney***, one who specializes in estate planning. I used an Estate Planning Attorney in my own estate planning.

This book is intended to help you prepare your information and financial data and gather what you will need to have a constructive meeting with an estate attorney.

I have no connections with any company mentioned in this book except possibly as a customer. I receive no compensation from any company for mentioning their name or their products. The only exception to this is www.moneyactionplan.com and www.neimaur.com, of which I am a principal partner of both.

Any books I mention are books I have read and used in my planning process.

Finally, nothing can prevent a reader from making incorrect decisions about their money and estate planning decisions. I certainly have made my share of incorrect decisions. What is presented in this book should help you arrive at the correct decisions in conjunction with your attorney.

What You Will Learn

Here is what you will learn in this book:

1. First, we will look briefly at what it means to get your estate ready to make it easier and less expensive on your heirs.

2. We will explain the items you absolutely need for estate planning and then we will go into detail in each of the areas presented.

3. You will learn the various components of an estate plan that you should consider for yourself.

4. You will learn about the various decisions you will need to make to formulate your estate plan.

5. You will also learn the various methods for

transferring assets to your heirs even starting before your death.

6. You will learn everything you will need to take with you to a qualified estate attorney so that your estate is prepared, and your heirs will need to do as little as possible.

7. Finally, we will tie all this into the Money Action Plan System (MAP) and the NEW Estate Planning System (EPS) so you will know how the system can help you in this. As with the other books, neither the MAP nor the EPS is needed for your success in planning for your estate, but it may make it easier.

So, first let's look at what estate planning really means and what you need to do to get ready for it.

Getting Ready

The subject of planning your estate can be closely linked with your retirement planning. There is, however, a very different objective.

In retirement planning, you are primarily concerned with having enough income to cover your expenses during your retirement years. This may require the services of an accountant or Certified Professional Accountant (CPA) or a financial planning professional such as a Chartered Financial Analyst (CFA) or Certified Financial Planner (CFP).

In estate planning, you are primarily concerned with what will become of your money, investments, personal property, real estate and other assets upon your death. This may require the services of an attorney who specializes in estate planning. You should be aware that there are many kinds of attorneys available. Most have some specialty which is the majority of their business and how they make their living. I'm sure you have heard of many of these specialties, corporate attorneys, criminal defense attorneys, labor attorneys, real estate attorneys, personal injury attorneys, etc. What you really need for estate planning is an attorney who specializes in estate planning. The reason for this is that if it is their only business, they tend to be more up to date on the legal matters concerning estate law and planning.

To prepare for planning your estate, there are several actions you should take as soon as possible.

Estate Planning – The Basics

FIRST, you should consolidate your investment accounts so that you have fewer accounts to deal with in the planning process. This can help streamline the entire process and make it easier for you to make changes in the future if the need arises.

SECOND, set up a record keeping system that a third party can understand and will be able to navigate when the time comes. The third party I'm referring to here can be almost anyone who is appointed by you or the probate court to perform any actions in connection with your estate. They must be able to find the records that are needed to settle your estate. There will be more about these records in another chapter.

THIRD, be sure there are specific instructions as to where to find everything that will be needed.

FOURTH, simplify wherever possible so the settlement of your estate can be carried out as quickly as possible.

FIFTH, learn the Terminology in the next chapter so that you will understand what this book is trying to explain and, more importantly, so you will be able to understand your attorney.

I should point out that no one has to have an estate plan. Federal and state laws provide for the administration of an estate if a person dies without any estate planning documents. However, you do not necessarily want the laws to take over and administer your estate. The probate laws do not necessarily reflect what you want done with your money and possessions. You need to have a plan that addresses those issues.

You can find an estate planning attorney for your

area at the following site:

American Academy of Estate Planning Attorneys

http://www.aaepa.com/

Estate Planning – The Basics

Terminology

The following are terms that you should be familiar with regarding estate planning so you can have a constructive meeting with an estate planning attorney.

Will

A will is a legal document that specifies in writing the desires of a person for the distribution of his or her property after their death. A will can be as simple as "I leave all my worldly possessions to my wife." It can also be a lot more complicated. For anything but the simplest will, an estate attorney should be consulted.

Forms for creating a will can be purchased in most stationary stores and there is also software available that will help you create a will.

Regardless of how you create your will, you should have a qualified estate attorney review it for the proper legal structure. This will help avoid any problems with your will after your death.

Also, in some states you are allowed to register your will through the secretary of state or your local probate court. Check with your secretary of state or probate court to see if your state allows this. This is done by filling out a form, paying a fee and then leaving a sealed copy of your will with them. Your attorney can take care of this for you, or you can do it yourself. Once this is done, only your executor will be able to access the information after your death.

Trust

There are two types of trusts: the living trust and the testamentary trust.

Living Trusts

A living trust (inter vivos) – is a written document which provides for an individual's assets to be put in the name of the trust with the individual (testator) named as Trustee. These assets can still be used for the benefit of the trust owner (testator) or Trustee until the person's death. Then they are transferred to the beneficiaries according to the terms of the trust. In the case of married couples, both can be named as Trustees of the Trust and the Trust can control what happens upon the death of one of them. If the Trustee is an individual, he or she would name a successor trustee who would be responsible for carrying out the terms of the trust.

Testamentary Trusts

A testamentary trust is a trust that takes effect after the testator's death. This trust would specify how the testator's assets are to be distributed.

Reasons for setting up a Trust

The primary reasons for having a trust are as follows:

Estate Planning

> Under the terms of a trust, specific requests can be made, and additional trustees can be designated for individuals who are named as beneficiaries of the trust. This may be necessary if the named beneficiary is under age 18, is incapacitated, or is not trusted to spend the money wisely.

Tax Planning

> In some cases, the taxes on a trust can be lower as compared to other means of

transferring assets. This would have to be determined by your attorney based on your individual circumstances.

Privacy

The terms of a trust are private while a will is a public document and the probate of the will is also public information.

Testator

Any person who has a valid will in effect at the time of their death.

Executor

An executor is a person who is responsible for carrying out the terms of a will or trust or otherwise settling the issues of an estate upon the death of the person. In the case where there is no will, the state will administer the estate and appoint an executor to gather all the assets and decide, under terms of the law, who will benefit from the estate. Usually, the assets are distributed to the surviving spouse and children. If you want your spouse to receive everything or the majority of your estate, you need to have a will or a trust.

The executor of a will can be a spouse, other family member or friend, most commonly being a child or a parent, or may be a legal representative, such as your estate attorney. An executor is not required to have expertise, or even experience, in dealing with financial or probate matters, but should be honest, diligent, and impartial, as he is acting on behalf of another person.

They might want to consider working with a qualified estate attorney on the administration of the estate.

Beneficiary - Primary and Secondary

A beneficiary is exactly what it says - someone or some organization who will benefit from something else. Where money is concerned, a beneficiary can be named on your checking and savings accounts, your life insurance policies, your investment accounts, your Individual Retirement Accounts (IRA), your 401K and other tax deferred retirement accounts and your personal property such as your car.

In a will (as defined), you can name the beneficiaries for all your personal property. However, be aware that **a beneficiary named on a specific account overrides any designation made in the will**. For instance, if you name your spouse as the beneficiary of your IRA with the company holding your IRA account and then name your children as the beneficiaries in your will, your spouse will get the funds upon your death. The direct beneficiary you named with the investment company overrides the beneficiary you named in your will.

If you are setting up a will or a trust, it is recommended that you review the direct beneficiaries you have named on all your accounts and make any changes necessary.

A secondary beneficiary is named in case the first beneficiary has predeceased the decedent. The secondary beneficiary, in this case, would receive nothing unless the primary beneficiary has already died.

Decedent

When an attorney talks about the decedent, it simply means the person who has died or whose death will trigger the terms of the will or the trust.

Bequest

A bequest is something that you give to another person, organization or charity in your will or trust after you die.

Any bequest can be one of four types.

1. From the estates general assets
2. From an explicit source, i.e. A checking or savings account, a named mutual fund, etc.
3. A specific item of property, i.e., a car, a painting, a diamond ring, etc.
4. A percentage of the remainder of the estate after all debts and expenses are paid.

IRA - Individual Retirement Account

An IRA is an account set up at a financial institution that allows an individual to save for retirement using before tax or after-tax dollars on a tax-deferred basis. There are three main types of IRAs, and each has different rules and benefits.

Traditional IRA

> This provides a way to save for retirement that gives you tax advantages. Contributions you make to a traditional IRA may be fully or partially deductible, depending on your circumstances. Generally, amounts in your traditional IRA (including earnings and gains) are not taxed until distributed.

Roth IRA

> A Roth IRA is a retirement plan under US

law that is generally not taxed, provided certain conditions are met. Contributions are made with after tax money and your money can grow tax-free, also with tax-free withdrawals during retirement.

Rollover IRA

A rollover occurs when you withdraw cash or other assets from one eligible retirement plan and contribute all or part of it, within 60 days, to another eligible retirement plan. A Rollover IRA is created by moving eligible assets from an employer-sponsored plan, such as a 401(k) or 403(b), into an IRA.

Power of Attorney

The term Power of Attorney can take many forms

as follows.

General Power of Attorney

This document gives someone designated by you control of all your affairs in the event of your death or incapacity for any reason. This should be included in your estate plan so that someone can handle your affairs after your death without having to go to court to have someone appointed.

Special Power of Attorney

This document gives someone designated by you certain powers in the event of your death or incapacity. This may include only the power to continue to pay your bills, for instance.

Medical or Health Care Power of Attorney

This document gives someone designated by you

the power to make medical decisions for you in the case where you are unable to make them yourself, for instance, if you are unconscious due to an accident or illness. This can also be used if you are mentally incompetent to make your own decisions, but this designation may require a court ruling to declare you mentally incompetent.

Durable Power of Attorney

Any of the previous three powers of attorney can be durable. This means that it has a provision that keeps it in effect, i.e., there is no expiration date.

Gift and Gift Tax - (definition from IRS)

The gift tax is a tax on the transfer of property by one individual to another while receiving nothing, or less than full value, in return. The tax applies whether the donor intends the transfer to be a gift or not.

Lifetime Gift Tax Exemption: The lifetime gift tax exemption is the total amount of gifts you can give over your lifetime without having to pay a gift tax. The lifetime gift tax exemption is the same as the estate tax exemption which is $12.92 million for 2023.

The general rule is that any gift is a taxable gift. However, there are many exceptions to this rule. These are explained in more detail in the chapter Methods of Transferring your assets.

Estate Tax

ESTATE TAX RULES FOR THE UNITED STATES

Most relatively simple estates (cash, publicly traded securities, lesser amounts of other easily valued assets, and no special deductions or elections, or jointly held property) do not require the filing of an estate tax return.

In the United States, the estate tax is a tax on the transfer of property upon the death of the owner. Here are some basic rules for estate taxes in the United States:

Exemption: For 2023, the estate tax exemption is $12.92 million. This means that an estate worth less than $12.92 million is not subject to estate taxes.

Estate Tax Rate: If the estate is worth more than the exemption amount, estate taxes will be owed. The estate tax rate is based on a graduated scale that starts at 18% and goes up to 40%.

Estate Tax Returns:

The executor of the estate is responsible for filing an estate tax return if the estate is worth more than the exemption amount. The estate tax return is due nine months after the date of death.

Estate Tax Planning:

Estate planning can help reduce the amount of estate taxes owed. This can include setting up trusts, making charitable donations, and taking advantage of annual gift tax exclusions.

It's important to note that estate tax rules can be complex, and you should consult with a tax professional and/or an estate planning attorney if you have questions or concerns about estate taxes.

Components of an Estate Plan

Your Assets

A list of all your assets, everything you own in whole or in part, is essential to a comprehensive estate plan. This means that you need to **have up-to-date statements for all your investment accounts, checking accounts, savings accounts, certificates of deposit,** etc.

Assets also include all your real estate holdings (homes, land, other buildings). You will need the address of each of these and the deeds if you plan to put them in a trust. Your estate attorney will facilitate the transfer of the deed to the trust.

You also have many personal assets that need to be considered. Items such as cars, boats, snowmobiles, motor homes, are usually valuable enough so that you may want to bequeath them to certain members of your family or friends.

Finally, you may have Intellectual Property, such as copyrights, patents, personal and business websites and social media accounts. These all have to be considered in your estate plan.

Your Distribution Plan

This is your plan for the distribution of your assets after your death. It can include a will, trust, beneficiary designations, and a Letter of Instruction.

For most people, the primary factor will be to provide security for a surviving spouse first before any other considerations.

Letter of Instruction

A Letter of Instruction can include the following:

Your Funeral Plan for yourself

If you have very specific ideas about your funeral and burial arrangements, these must be stated in writing, or they might be ignored. This can include specific details about the type of service you want, "in lieu of flowers" instructions, wish to be cremated or buried, where the service and/or burial should take place, what should be done with your ashes. This should also include instructions regarding any burial plot that you have purchased, where it is and who to contact.

Your Obituary written by you.

One of the most overlooked items is your obituary. Often it is a rushed creation just to get it in the local paper so your friends will know about your death.

You should take the opportunity to write your own obituary so that all the high points of your life are included. Not all your family members, including your children, will be aware of everything you have done or participated in during your lifetime. This is your chance to make it known.

Included in this should be the names and locations of your spouse, children, aunts, uncles, grandparents, grandchildren, cousins, etc. who you want to mention.

I have actually read some obituaries and been really surprised by some of the items that I didn't even know about and especially who some of the person's relatives were.

Specific Bequests

This is the place to mention bequests that are not mentioned in your will or trust. These can be specific instructions regarding your art collection, baseball card collection, family heirlooms, antiques, jewelry, etc.

Take the time to be sure everyone knows your wishes on these items that are not specifically covered in your will or trust.

What you must decide

When you die, you will most likely have many possessions. The primary purpose of an estate plan is to decide in advance what will happen to all those assets after your death.

In a nutshell,

<u>YOU</u> MUST DECIDE

WHO GETS WHAT

AND HOW

AND WHEN.

The assets you need to consider can be defined in the following categories:

Money or Cash

You will undoubtedly have a checking account, maybe a savings account or other items that could be considered cash. Who will receive this or have access to this after your death? If this is a joint account, the other account holder automatically has access to the account after your death. Be sure this is the person you want to have access to the account.

Investments

You may have investments in stocks, bonds, mutual funds in either or both a brokerage account and a retirement account. You have to provide for the distribution of these after your death.

Personal Property

One thing that many people don't think about is their personal property. This includes items such as your clothes, books, jewelry, tools, furniture, electronics, bicycles, cars, motorcycles, motor homes, skimobiles, skidoos, atv's, personal art collections, family heirlooms, hobby collections, etc. There are many items that you might want to give to a specific person and estate planning is the way to do that.

Real Estate

The distribution of your real estate holdings is a very important consideration in your estate plan. This includes your primary residence, vacation homes, time shares, land, etc.

Business Property

Any property that you own as a business or for rental purposes is considered business property.

Shares of a Business

If you own all or part of a business, you will have to provide for the continuation or sale of the business in your estate plan.

Intellectual Property

Copyrights

If you have written a book or designed a website, drawn pictures that are published, among other things, you probably have a copyright on that item. Copyrights can be automatic just by means of the publishing process or you can register your copyright.

Either way, if you do own copyrights, you may want to provide for them in your estate plan.

Patents

If you invented anything and had it patented, you own the patent for this product whether or not it was ever produced and sold. These should be provided for in your estate plan.

Royalties

If you receive royalties on published works, you will need to provide for the distribution of these. Usually, the royalties go with whomever is given the copyrights to the published material.

Websites

If you have any websites that you own, you should list them so that your executor knows that something has to be done with them. Also, on the For MY Eyes Only form, list the administrator sign on for the site so your executor or someone else will be able to get to it for updates, additions, etc. or to close down the site if it is no longer needed.

Social Media Sites

As with websites, you should list all your social media accounts. These include Facebook, Instagram, TikTok, LinkedIn, YouTube (if you post videos), WhatsApp, Twitter, Snapchat, Pinterest, Reddit, Tumblr.

There are, undoubtedly, many that are not listed here. New ones are being created all the time and old ones go out of business.

As with the websites, your executor or someone else, needs the logon IDs and passwords for each of these sites to possibly close it if necessary. These should be listed on the For MY Eyes Only form. There is no reason for your estate attorney to have this unless they eventually become the executor of your estate.

Estate Planning – The Basics

Methods of transferring your assets

Beneficiary designations

On bank accounts, a beneficiary can be designated so that the person designated can continue to pay your bills after your death. This is common practice and usually it is a spouse if there is one.

Beneficiaries can also be designated on stocks, bonds, mutual funds, savings bonds, etc.

Will

A will is one document for recording what you want to happen to your personal possessions. Everyone should, at the very least, have a will executed by a qualified attorney. This may help reduce some family squabbling over your estate and will give the probate court a good idea of what your wishes are. **Beneficiary Designations** override a **Will**. Some people think an updated **will** is all you need. Your **will** or trust **will** not **override** what is named in the **beneficiary designation** on a checking or savings account, life insurance policy, annuity, or retirement account (like an IRA or 401k plan). You need to change the beneficiary on these to name the trust (if you have one) so that your trust instructions will control who gets what.

Trusts

Trusts are another form of providing for the disbursement of your estate. A Living Trust allows you to put your major assets into the trust name with you and your spouse named as trustees. The most common form is to have the trust pass to the surviving trustee(s) upon the death of one. Other secondary trustees can be designated, so that after the death of both primary trustees, the trust continues.

You should not try to organize a trust on your own unless you are a qualified estate attorney. Trust laws and organization is a specialized field. The major benefit is that it may save taxes on the estate and put you in a better position if you or your spouse need to enter a nursing home or long-term care facility.

Gifts before death

Before your death, you are allowed to give gifts to people and to charities up to a certain amount designated by the IRS and these gifts are tax free to you and the recipient. This year, 2023, that amount is $17,000.

Directly from the IRS website here are the Eight

Tips to Determine if Your Gift is Taxable.

"If you gave money or property to someone as a gift, you may owe federal gift tax. Many gifts are not subject to the gift tax, but the IRS offers the following eight tips about gifts and the gift tax.

1. Most gifts are not subject to the gift tax. For example, there is usually no tax if you give a gift to your spouse or to a charity. If you make a gift to someone else, the gift tax usually does not apply until the value of the gifts you give that person exceeds the annual exclusion for the year. For 2023, the annual exclusion is $17,000.

2. Gift tax returns do not need to be filed unless you give someone, other than your spouse, money or property worth more than the annual exclusion for that year.

3. Generally, the person who receives your gift will not have to pay any federal gift tax because of it. Also, that person will not have to pay income tax on the value of the gift received.

4. Making a gift does not ordinarily affect your federal income tax. You cannot deduct the value of gifts you make (other than deductible charitable contributions).

5. The general rule is that any gift is a taxable gift. However, there are many exceptions to this rule. The following gifts are not taxable gifts:

    • Gifts that do not exceed the annual exclusion for the calendar year

    • Tuition or medical expenses you pay directly to a medical or educational

institution for someone else
- Gifts to your spouse
- Gifts to a political organization for its use
- Gifts to charities.

6. You and your spouse can make a gift up to $34,000 ($17,000 from each of you in 2023) to a third party without making a taxable gift. The gift can be considered as made one-half by you and one-half by your spouse. If you split a gift you made, you must file a gift tax return to show that you and your spouse agree to use gift splitting. You must file a Form 709, United States Gift (and Generation-Skipping Transfer) Tax Return, even if half of the split gift is less than the annual exclusion.

7. You must file a gift tax return on Form 709,

if any of the following apply:

- You gave gifts to at least one person (other than your spouse) that are more than the annual exclusion for the year.
- You and your spouse are splitting a gift.
- You gave someone (other than your spouse) a gift of a future interest that he or she cannot actually possess, enjoy, or receive income from until sometime in the future.
- You gave your spouse an interest in property that will terminate due to a future event.

8. You do not have to file a gift tax return to report gifts to political organizations and gifts made by paying someone's tuition or medical expenses."

Foundations

A private foundation can be started by anyone and contributions to the foundation are generally tax deductible. There are rules about how much you have to pay out each year based on the foundation's assets.

Private foundations are:

- Independent legal entities
- Organized exclusively for charitable, educational, religious, scientific or literary purposes.
- Usually controlled and funded by a single individual, family or business (not public fundraising)

If you are interested in starting your own foundation for tax or estate purposes, you must contact a qualified attorney to do so. The following website, www.foundationsource.com, may also be able to help in this.

Meeting with Your Estate Attorney

The following forms are essential for your meeting with you Estate Attorney:

Personal Information Form for all the information about you; your full name, your spouse's full name, all your children, other relatives and friends who may be part of your estate.

A Cash Accounts List - any checking, savings or other bank accounts.

An Investment Assets List with a section to make notes about your intended distribution of the assets.

Real Estate List - for listing your real estate holdings (your main home, any other homes owned (vacation, rentals), business and commercial buildings, etc.)

Copyright List - a blank form for you to list copyrights in your name.

Patent List - a blank form for you to list patents in your name.

Website List - list any websites you own.

Social Media Accounts List - list all your social media accounts.

Business Owned List - to list businesses owned entirely or partially by you.

Specific Estate Bequests List - to list any asset you want to go to a specific person or organization.

Other Assets - for listing assets you don't want included in your estate plan for whatever reason.

For MY Eyes Only List for logons and passwords

to websites, social media accounts, etc.

All these forms and others are available in the Money Action Plan Software or can be downloaded for completion offline.

Estate Planning – The Basics

For What It's Worth

Here's how I did my estate planning.

I immediately got an attorney who specializes in estate planning. This relieved me of the majority of the planning and only required me to gather together the information I needed to take to the meeting with the attorney. I used the forms that I developed for this book.

My wife and I decided to have a Living Trust set up to contain all our significant assets so that none of these assets were individually bequeathed to anyone directly but only through the trust document.

Because IRA and other types of accounts specifically designed for retirement cannot be renamed into the trust name, we changed the beneficiary on each of those accounts to be the living trust. That way, when either or both of us die, the money assets will become part of the trust and then be divided according to the terms of the trust as defined by us.

Here's what we took to the estate attorney at our first meeting with them.

- Personal Data Sheets

- Deeds from our real estate holdings (a main house and a second vacation home)

- Titles to our cars

- Statements of how we wanted the assets distributed when one of us dies and then when the other one dies.

- Statements from all cash accounts (checking, savings, certificates of deposit, etc.).

- Most Recent statements from all of our investment accounts including the IRA, 401K, etc. and personal non-retirement investment accounts.

- Documents regarding the business which we own, and which will need to be distributed.

- Information about any copyrights (books) and patents (inventions) owned.

- Information about royalties due.

- Business Organization Documents

Our estate planning attorney then drew up the necessary Living Trust Documents to provide for our wishes.

In our case, it was really straight forward. When one of us dies, the other becomes the sole Trustee of the trust for his or her life. We have two sons who will share equally in the estate with the exception of specific bequests made by each of us to other people and organizations. This will be accomplished by spitting our Living Trust into two equal Living Trusts in each of their names with each of them as sole Trustee, upon the death of both of us.

Each of them can then carry on the trust and get regular income from it or cash in everything, take the money and pay the taxes. This is not recommended for tax purposes. They are also free to name other Trustees for their Living Trust, such as their children.

Your own trust may be more complicated based on the number of children you have, other family members, other people you want to leave something to, the amount of your assets, business interests, etc.

Forms for Estate Planning

These Estate Planning Forms are available for download at www.moneyactionplan.com in the download section. These forms are in PDF format so you will need Adobe Reader (a free application) to be able to view, read and print these. You won't be able to complete them online after downloading.

You can also download the NEW Estate Planning System which provides all the forms in a format to be completed in the spreadsheets and then printed for your records and for meeting with an estate planning attorney.

Rather than taking up a lot of space showing you blank forms, I have taken a different approach in this book. I'll show you the Title and Column Headings for each form and you are free to make up your own forms or download the forms or download the Estate Planning System from the website which has all the forms.

These forms are:

Cash Accounts List

A Cash Accounts List to list any checking, savings or other bank accounts.

The column headers are:

- Account Name
- Account #
- Account Owner
- Balance (current)
- As of Date (of current balance)
- Beneficiary – this is important because any beneficiary named on the account will override any beneficiary designation in a will or trust.
- Have Statement Y/N – do you have a current statement for this account?

- Copy Attached Y/N – have you attached a copy of the statement to this form?

Investment Assets List

An Investment Assets List for all your stock, bond, mutual funds, certificates of deposit and any other cash investment. This should include any retirement accounts such as IRAs, 401Ks, 457Bs or other accounts you contribute to through your employer or former employer.

The column headers are:

- Account Name
- Account # / Fund #
- Account Owner
- Balance (current)
- As of Date (of current balance)
- Beneficiary – this is important because any beneficiary named on the account will override any beneficiary designation in a will or trust.

- Have Statement Y/N – do you have a current statement for this account?
- Copy Attached Y/N – have you attached a copy of the statement to this form?

Real Estate List

Real Estate List - this is for listing your real estate holdings (your main home, any other homes owned (vacation, rentals), business and commercial buildings owned, land, etc.)

The column headers are:

- Property Name
- Property Address
- Owner(s) – of the property
- Valuation – how much is this property worth?
- Deed Ownership Form – how is the deed worded as to the ownership of this property? This may impact some parts of your estate plan, so your attorney needs to know about this. Some possibilities are:

- o Joint Tenancy
- o Joint tenancy with rights of survivorship (JTWROS)
- o Tenancy in Common
- o Community Property
- Have Deed Y/N – do you have a copy of the deed?
- Copy Attached Y/N – have you attached a copy of the deed?

Copyright List

Copyright List - this is a blank form for you to list your copyrights.

The column headers are:

- Name of Work
- Published / Copyright Date
- Copyright Owner
- Copyright Date
- Copies Sold or Distributed

- Valuation
- Have Written Copyright Y/N
- Copy Attached Y/N

Patent List

Patent List - this is a form for you to list any patents that you own.

The column headers are:

- Name of Patent
- Details (if required)
- Patent Owner
- Patent Date
- Valuation
- Have Final Patent Form Y/N
- Copy Attached Y/N

Websites Owned List

List any websites you own solely or partially.

The column headers are:

- Name and URL of Website
- Details (if required)
- Owner(s)
- Type of Website
- What is it used for?

Social Media Accounts

List any social media accounts (facebook, twitter, linkedin, instagram, tiktok, etc.

The column headers are:

- Name on account
- Platform (facebook, twitter, etc.)
- Owner
- What is it used for?

Business Owned

Business Owned List – this is for listing your full or partial ownership in any business and are named in a partnership, LLC or Corp agreement.

The column headers are:

- Legal Business Name
- Name(s) of all Owners
- Percent Owned (by owner)
- Address of Owner
- Phone #
- Email
- Valuation (of each owner share or at least your share)
- Have Business Org Document Y/N
- Copy Attached Y/N

Other Assets

List any other assets you think should be a part of your estate, such as specific items of jewelry, art collections, cars, classic cars, motor homes, etc. This is for assets of any value that are not listed on other forms.

The column headers are:

- Item or Account
- More details (if required)
- Owner(s), if necessary
- Estimated Value or Appraisal
- NOTES

Specific Estate Bequests

Specific Estate Bequests List to list any asset you want to go to a specific person or organization.

The column headers are:

- Item or Account
- Details (if required) – use this if the item or account is not clear.
- Owner(s) of item or account
- Estimated Value or Appraisal
- Who should get it – Who do you want to receive this item or account after your death. If it is an account, name that person or

organization as the primary beneficiary on the account.

Personal Data Sheet

Personal Data Sheet – this form is for gathering all the personal data that your estate attorney may need to complete your estate plan.

```
Personal Data Sheet
Full Legal Name 1                              Date of Birth
Full Legal Name 2                              Date of Birth
Married Y/N
Permanent Address
Phone(s)
Email(s)
Children (Full Legal Names):
        1                 Date of birth        Address         Phone
        2                 Date of birth        Address         Phone
        3                 Date of birth        Address         Phone
        4                 Date of birth        Address         Phone
        5                 Date of birth        Address         Phone
        6                 Date of birth        Address         Phone
        7                 Date of birth        Address         Phone
        8                 Date of birth        Address         Phone
        9                 Date of birth        Address         Phone
       10                 Date of birth        Address         Phone

Other Beneficiaries (Full Legal Names):
        1                 Date of Birth        Address         Phone
        2                 Date of Birth        Address         Phone
        3                 Date of Birth        Address         Phone
        4                 Date of Birth        Address         Phone
        5                 Date of Birth        Address         Phone

Person to be Named Executor of Estate (Full Legal Name):
        1                 Address              Phone
        2                 Address              Phone
```

Other forms you should consider are:

- Power of Attorney

Because powers of attorney can be state-specific, it is not possible to present one that would be good in all instances and all states. Refer to the following site for information about the power of attorney form you may need or talk to your attorney about this. (https://powerofattorney.com/). This includes all types of powers of attorney, including medical forms.

Some of the forms on that website are fillable pdf forms which means you can fill them out online and then print them out. I do recommend that any legal form you complete online should be reviewed by an attorney.

Estate Planning – The Basics

How can the Money Action Plan Software help you with your Estate Plan?

NEW Software! With this revision of the book, we are also announcing that there is now a completely separate Estate Planning System that you can download from www.moneyactionplan.com. All the forms provided in the full Money Action Plan System are now available in the separate Estate Planning Software.

If you don't think you need the full Money Action Plan System which includes Budgeting and Money Management, you can download the Estate Planning System just for the purpose of getting ready for a meeting with an estate planning attorney.

All the forms are described in the Forms for Estate Planning chapter.

Conclusion

I hope you can see from the activities detailed in this book that advance preparation for your estate planning is essential to getting the most from your visit with your estate planning attorney and being confident that your plan will carry out your desired actions after your death.

Estate Planning – The Basics

About the Author

Neil Bryan is a successful business consultant. He is a graduate of the University of Redlands in California with both a Bachelor's and a Master's Degree (MBA) in Business Administration.

Along the way he has designed and used paper forms as well as Excel spreadsheets and Access databases to manage and control his business ventures. He is an accomplished systems designer and programmer who designed many specialized business systems including a restaurant management system for a privately owned chain of restaurants, a booking system for a bus tour company and a routing system for a package delivery service.

He has also been involved in many implementations of large-scale computer systems using Oracle Applications, with a specialty in Financials, Procure-to-Pay and Order to Cash systems. His other specialty is Business Process Reengineering, i.e., redesigning business processes to streamline them, thereby reducing costs and increasing profit. These projects have taken him throughout the United States with one project in Japan.

Currently he is retired and divides his time with his wife, Maureen, between his summer home in Massachusetts, his winter home in Arizona and traveling the world.

When they aren't traveling, he spends much of his time sorting through his software and forms trying to bring the most practical of these to the general public so others can benefit from them. This book is one of those efforts.

Other Neil Bryan Books

All these books are available at:

www.amazon.com

www.amazon.com/author/neilbryan

www.neilbryan.com

Profit-izing Your Business: Squeezing the most out of everyday business activities by revising and streamlining your processes.

Quick Reads for Commuters and Others: Stories, poems, essays, and other writings to read in fifteen minutes or less.

Money Action Plan Series:

1. *Budgeting and Money Management – The Basics:* A lifelong plan for budgeting and

managing your money. This includes free downloadable software.

2. *Keep More of What You Earn*: This book provides all the details of how to review and maximize your income and how to review and minimize your expenses. It also includes a year's worth of forms for creating a manual budget.

3. *Investing - The Basics*: A step by step investment plan starter plan.

4. *Retirement Planning - The Basics*: Step by step planning your retirement.

5. *Estate Planning - The Basics*: Step by step planning your estate.

Rental Property Records Book: Two sizes: 6 x 9 inches and 8 ½ x 11 inches - Keep all your annual records for up to 12 rental properties in one book.

Meeting Notes Journal: For those who still like to jot things down during meetings or conference calls.

Coursework Notes Journal: Organize your class and work schedule for academic success!

The Everyday Planning Book: Plan anything you need or want to do.

Write NOW! Handbook for Organizing, Writing and Formatting your book.

Write Your First Book in 30 Days: This book is about writing a book using the book being written as examples. See the entire process and this book is the finished work.

Estate Planning – The Basics

Neil Bryan WEBSITES:

www.neimaur.com - my corporate website with links to all my other sites:

www.neilbryan.com - my personal writer's blog

Mentorship.neilbryan.com - my Author Mentorship Program

www.moneyactionplan.com - the Money Action Plan (MAP) System

Visit the MAP website to learn more about the MAP system, download a complete introduction to the system, get access to the software and forms. The site is periodically updated with new articles on the subject matter.

www.wordstolivewith.com - ecommerce website selling t-shirts and mugs with friend's designs.

Estate Planning – The Basics

Neil Bryan Software

Available for download at

www.moneyactionplan.com.

- *Money Action Plan System* – a complete system for Budgeting, Money Management, Investing, Retirement Planning and Estate Planning.

- *Retirement Planning System* – all the retirement planning parts of the full Money Action Plan System together in an enhanced stand-alone format.

- *Estate Planning System* - all the estate planning parts of the full Money Action Plan System together in an enhanced stand-alone format.

www.ingramcontent.com/pod-product-compliance
Lightning Source LLC
Chambersburg PA
CBHW060400190526
45169CB00002B/684